Soul Winning

Inspiration for Leading
People to Jesus!

Daniel King

Soul Winning

Soul Winning: Inspiration for Leading People to Jesus!
ISBN #: 1-931810-03-6

Copyright 2006 by:
Daniel King
King Ministries
PO Box 701113
Tulsa, OK 74170-1113 USA
1-877-431-4276
daniel@kingministries.com

Foreword by Peter Youngren

Inspiration! Passion! Joy! These three words describe Soul Winning.

The author motivates the reader through Jesus' own words and actions, while at the same time drawing on inspirational statements from some of the "greats" in the history of revival and soul winning.

I have seen Daniel King in action and the book exudes the same passion for people that you notice when you spend time with the author. Whether standing on a large platform, preaching to a vast multitude, or reaching out to one person, Daniel cares for people and is willing to do whatever it takes to bring the gospel to those who need it the most.

Jesus said, "there is joy in heaven" when a person repents. That same joy and enthusiasm is a must in our soul-winning work. Without this, evangelism becomes a drudgery, a mere religious obligation.

Recently Daniel and I spent some time together in Congo. He shared how at the age of fifteen, he read a book where the author encouraged young people to set a goal to earn $1,000,000 before the age of thirty. Daniel re-interpreted the message and determined to win 1,000,000, people to Christ before the age of thirty...and he is well on his way.

Jesus is our role model. He ministered to Jews, Samaritans, and Romans without discrimination. Soul winning 101 will challenge the reader to reach out to every sphere of society, with the simplicity the gospel. The Apostle Paul faced reluctance from the Jews—the people of the law - who found the gospel to be a stumbling block. The Greek—the philosophers of that day - had their own objections; they considered

3

the gospel foolishness. The apostle's response was clear – "to us who believe (the gospel) it is the power of God."

This confidence in the gospel is evident in Soul Winning. Regardless of background or religion when a person chooses to believe, the power of God manifests. The gospel—carries an iron-clad guarantee to work for everyone who will believe it.

Someone noted, "When all is said and done, a whole lot more was said than ever done." While this book gives a wealth of information; it will also stir others to Holy Spirit empowered action.

Introduction:

Dear Friend,

I am passionate about soul winning. My goal is to win 1,000,000 people to Jesus every year of my life.

Souls are the most precious treasures...in heaven...in hell...and here on earth.

Why am I so passionate about bringing people to Jesus? Several years ago, I was in the country of Jamaica swimming in a pool when I noticed smoke coming from a panel on the edge of the pool. Stupidly, I swam over to investigate. ZAP! An underwater light shocked me. I pulled myself out and limped away thanking God I had not been killed. Suddenly, I remembered that all my friends were still in the water. I started yelling at them to get out. Some of them thought it was a practical joke, but I was so concerned for their safety that I refused to give up until I had saved everyone's life.

God spoke to me, **"Daniel, I want you to save people from hell with the same passion you saved your friends from the pool."**

My experience in the pool illustrates what Christianity is like. Once God saves us, we have a choice, do we just walk away thanking God, or do we go back to save others who are still in a dangerous situation?

Are you glad the person who led you to the Lord was excited about soul winning? Now, it is your turn to help someone else.

Soul Winning

I believe every Christian should be passionate about soul winning. This book will inspire you to win souls in your neighborhood, in your workplace, in your family, in your city, and around the world.

There are only three options for the **Serious Soul Winner**

Go and Say,
or Stay and Pray,
or help Pay the Way!

Hopefully, this book will help you discover your part in bringing the world to Jesus.

Your partner in Soul Winning,

Daniel King

The greatest treasure in HEAVEN is a soul!

The only thing God values is a soul.

"The glory of God is man fully alive."
- St. Irenaeus

Despite the golden streets, beautiful mansions, gemstone foundations, and pearly gates, the most valuable object in heaven is a soul who has chosen to love God.

Why are souls so precious to God? Since every human being has free-choice, a soul who chooses to love God is infinitely cherished by Him.

"I tell you, there is rejoicing in the presence of the angels of God over one sinner who repents." (Luke 15:10)

"God has two thrones: One is in the highest heaven, and the other is in the lowest heart."

Soul Winning

God can create anything He wants by speaking a word, except for a soul. When God created the world, He said, "Let there be light" and there was light. The only thing God cannot create out of thin air is a free agent who chooses to love Him.

It cost God nothing to create, but it cost Him everything to redeem.

"God said, "Let there be light," and there was light...the LORD God formed the man from the dust of the ground and breathed into his nostrils the breath of life, and the man became a living being." (Genesis 1:3; 2:7)

The saddest day in heaven was the day
Adam and Eve were separated from God by sin.
The happiest day in heaven was the day
Jesus made it possible for mankind to be restored to God.

"There is no trouble too great, no humiliation too deep, no suffering too severe, no love too strong, no labor too hard, no expense too large, but that it is worth it, if it is spent in the effort to win a soul"
- The Open Bible

God has paid an immeasurably high price for each soul - the blood of Jesus! This blood was shed on the cross to pay the redemption price for every sinner. No other commodity in the universe has ever commanded such a high purchase price.

"...the blood of Jesus, his Son, purifies us from all sin"
(1 John 1:7).

Just as the blood of American patriots purchased American freedom, so the blood of Jesus purchased eternal freedom.

"What you can do, you ought to do and what you ought to do by the help of God, DO!"

A soul was the only possession for which God was willing to sacrifice His only Son.

Jesus *"...redeemed my soul from going down to the pit"* (Job 33:28).

The greatest treasure in HELL is a soul!

Souls are the commodity of the universe.
God wants souls. Satan wants souls.
Eternal lives are what Satan and God are fighting over.

Soul Winning

"I tell you that in the same way there will be more rejoicing in heaven over one sinner who repents than over ninety-nine righteous persons who do not need to repent."
(Luke 15:7)

The only way Satan can hurt God is by stealing a soul.

"The thief comes only to steal and kill and destroy; I have come that they may have life, and have it to the full"
(John 10:10).

Every time a soul enters eternity, either Satan or God rejoices. If the soul goes to heaven God and all the angels throw a party. If the soul winds up in hell, Satan and all the demons throw a party.

"Do not be afraid of those who kill the body but cannot kill the soul. Rather, be afraid of the one who can destroy both soul and body in hell" (Matthew 10:28).

Redeeming a soul from Satan's grasp is the only way to hurt Satan.

"Friends don't let friends go to hell."
- Seen on a T-shirt

Spiritual warfare without soul winning is pointless. You can stomp up and down and pray all day but you have not won a spiritual battle until you have snatched a soul from Satan's grasp.

Soul Winning

The angels rejoice when a sinner gets saved, equally important to understand is that demons get angry each time a sinner comes to God. Demonic powers will use any weapon in their nasty arsenal in order to prevent a soul from getting saved.

"For our struggle is not against flesh and blood, but against the rulers, against the authorities, against the powers of this dark world and against the spiritual forces of evil in the heavenly realms." (Ephesians 6:12).

Satan's greatest attacks are against those who are winning souls from his evil kingdom.

"We must Plunder Hell to Populate Heaven!"
-Reinhard Bonnke

"There are no closed doors to the gospel, provided that, once you go through the door, you don't care whether or not you come back out." - Brother Andrew

The greatest treasure on EARTH is a soul!

God does not care about worldly wealth,
all He cares about are souls.

"The church of Jesus Christ is not a pleasure boat,
it is a lifeboat. From the captain to the cook,
all hands are needed on deck for soul saving."
- Reinhard Bonnke

In the hustle and bustle of life, we place great value on money, cars,
and houses; but when the Father looks down from heaven,
all He cares about are people.

"A church that does not seek the lost is lost itself."
- Reinhard Bonnke

A soul is worth far more than the accumulated wealth of the world. If you piled up all the world's wealth on one side of a balance and placed a soul on the other side, one single soul would outweigh the wealth of the entire world.

Jesus said, *"What good will it be for a man if he gains the whole world, yet forfeits his soul? Or what can a man give in exchange for his soul?"* (Matthew 16:26).

The greatest gift you can give God is your soul.

The second greatest gift you can give God is someone else's soul.

"Everyone who calls on the name of the Lord will be saved." (Acts 2:21)

"Those who win souls are wise." (Proverbs 11:30)

Soul Winning

Giving money or time to God has only two purposes. First, it is a way to show God your soul truly belongs to Him. Second, it is a way to help win more souls for the Kingdom of God.

> "You have one business on earth, to save souls; therefore, spend and be spent in this work."
> - John Wesley

You cannot take money or possessions with you to heaven. Souls are the only treasure you can take to heaven with you when you die.

> "In eternity there is nothing from this life that will have been more important than the people you and I reach for Christ."
> - Mike Downey

Many Christians do not reap harvests because they are planting seed into ministries that are not saving souls.
Only seed sown into the good ground of world evangelism will produce a harvest.

> "I will go down, if you will hold the rope."
> - William Carrey

Soul Winning

The greatest use for earthly treasure
is buying heavenly treasure.
The only way to trade earthly treasure
for heavenly treasure is by winning souls.

"That man is no fool who gives what he cannot
keep to gain what he cannot lose."
- Jim Elliot

Feeding the poor, taking care of the sick, building Bible schools, and starting churches is only worthwhile if it helps people go to heaven. A beautiful church building is useless if it is empty. God does not dwell in church buildings, He lives in the hearts of the souls who occupy church buildings.

"The supreme task of the Church
is the evangelization of the world."
- Oswald J. Smith

When you arrive in heaven, you will be judged based on the condition of your own soul, but you will be rewarded based on how many souls you bring to heaven with you.

Soul Winning

> "Jesus' passion drove him to the CROSS,
> now our passion drives us to the LOST!"
> - T.L. Osborn

The only economic indicator of success or failure in heaven will be the souls you bring with you. The jewels in your crown will be rewards for the numbers of souls you helped save.

> "GIVE ME SOULS OR I DIE!"
> - John Knox

> "Woe to me if I preach not the Gospel."
> - Paul the Apostle

All God really wants from you is your soul. He does not need your money, He desires your love. Giving money to God is just a way of letting Him know that He has all of your soul.

> "The glory of God, and, as our only means to glorifying Him, the salvation of human souls, is the real business of life."
> - C.S. Lewis

Winning souls is the greatest occupation available on earth.

"Surely there can be no deeper joy than that of saving souls."
- Lottie Moon

Winning souls is the only mission worth
investing your life (and wealth) in.
How many souls can you purchase with
your talent and resources?

A missionary society wrote to David Livingstone who was deep in the heart of Africa and asked, "Have you found a good road to where you are? If so, we want to know how to send other men to join you."

Livingstone wrote back: "If you have men who will come only if they know there is a good road, I don't want them. I want men who will come if there is no road at all."

Every soul on earth desperately thirsts for a relationship with God. There are millions of souls ready to accept God if only they will be told the truth about how to get to heaven.

"As the deer pants for streams of water,
so my soul pants for you, O God"
(Psalm 42:1)

Soul Winning

God's blessings are rewards for those who win souls. There is one level of blessing for those who have given their own soul to God, but there is an even greater level of blessing for those who lead other souls to God.

"If you read history you will find that the Christians who did the most for the present world were precisely those who thought most of the next. It is since Christians have largely ceased to think of the other world that they have become so ineffective in this." - C.S. Lewis

The only gift worth giving to God is a soul. Giving money towards soul winning is the greatest investment you can make. Soul winning is the only investment where a finite amount produces an infinite return.

"To know God's will is life's greatest treasure. To do God's will is Life's greatest pleasure."

Evangelism is not a task reserved for professional clergy, it is a job for every believer.

"World evangelization requires the whole Church to take the whole gospel to the whole world."
- The Lausanne Covenant

Soul Winning

Earthly wealth will never last,
heavenly wealth will never fade.

*"Store up for yourselves treasures in heaven,
where moth and rust do not destroy,
and where thieves do not break in and steal"*
(Matthew 6:20).

Those who GIVE towards preaching the gospel will receive the same
reward as those who preach the gospel.

*"The share of the man who stayed with the supplies is to be the
same as that of him who went down to the battle.
All will share alike."*
(1 Samuel 30:24).

With over six billion souls on earth,
the church must dream BIG, set BIG goals,
give BIG amounts of money, and do BIG things
in order to win as many souls as possible.

"God does not want nibblers of the possible,
but grabbers of the impossible."
- C.T. Studd

The time for small thinking is over.

> "We honor God when we ask for great things.
> It is a humiliating thing to think that we are satisfied
> with very small results."
> - D.L. Moody

When we give God our best, He gives us His best.

> "We never test the resources of God
> until we attempt the impossible."
> - D. L. Moody

There are millions of people dying every year who never had the opportunity to hear the Gospel. Meanwhile, there are millions of Christians who have never taken the opportunity to share the Gospel.

> "The gospel is good news only if it arrives in time."
> - Carl F. H. Henry

If you do not have a vision for reaching the lost, all the lives you could have saved will die an eternal death.

> *"Where there is no vision, the people perish"*
> (Proverbs 29:18).

Written goals are perhaps the greatest power in the universe. When you put pen to paper, ideas leave dreamland and enter the world of reality. So, what is your soul winning goal for your life? For this year? For today?

"And the LORD answered me, and said, Write the vision, and make it plain upon tables, that he may run that readeth it...it will surely come..." (Habakkuk 2:2-3 -KJV).

No vision has ever been big enough to satisfy
God's expectations
nor expensive enough to exhaust
His resources.

"Attempt great things for God.
Expect great things from God."
- William Carey

Vision draws resources like supermagnets attract metal.
The pull is irresistible, relentless, and overpowering.

"Visionaries are never willing to shelve God's vision simply because the resources appear to be unavailable...One of the most remarkable truths about vision is that when the vision is implemented, the result is creating, rather than consuming resources." - George Barna

To Infinity... and Beyond!

1. Every soul will live an infinite amount of time. *"Then they will go away to eternal punishment, but the righteous to eternal life."* Matthew 25:46

2. Every soul will experience an infinite amount of either pain or pleasure. *"The soul who sins is the one who will die"* (Ezekiel 18:20).

3. Every soul is infinitely precious to God. *"For God so loved the world that he gave his one and only Son, that whoever believes in him shall not perish but have eternal life"* (John 3:16).

4. God was willing to pay an infinite price for every soul. *"They that trust in their wealth, and boast themselves in the multitude of their riches; None of them can by any means redeem his brother, nor give to God a ransom for him: For the redemption of their soul is precious..."* (Psalm 49:6-8 - KJV).

5. The blood of Jesus is able to save an infinite number of souls. *"The blood of Jesus, his Son, purifies us from all sin."* (1 John 1:7).

6. Each soul is worth an infinite amount of trouble on our part. *"He who wins souls is wise"* (Proverbs 11:30).

7. A monetary gift towards soul winning instantly becomes infinitely valuable. *"Whoever sows generously will also reap generously"* (2 Corinthians 9:6).

Henry Ford once said, "I am looking for a lot of men with an infinite capacity for not knowing what cannot be done." I think God is looking for the same type of person.

WHO will reach them if not YOU?

As you go, preach!

The Bible says in Matthew 10:7, *"And as ye go, preach, saying, The kingdom of heaven is at hand" (KJV)*. Notice this verse does not say "When you arrive on the mission field, preach" or "On Sunday morning, when in a pulpit, preach." It says "as you go, preach."

In the original Greek language, these words are in the continuous present tense. This means we are supposed to preach the arrival of the kingdom everywhere we go. So, we could translate this verse for today's world, "As you go to the grocery store, preach" or "As you go to work, preach" or "As you attend your son's soccer game, preach."

If you want to catch fish, go where the fish are swimming!

We are to be fishers of men, not keepers of the aquarium.
- Mike Francen

Oswald J. Smith said, "Our duty is not done when we minister only to those who come into our churches. If they do not come, we have no choice but to go to them."

1. The job of the church is to win the lost.
2. The lost, for the most part, never enter our churches.
3. Therefore, it is up to us to take the gospel outside the walls of the church to where the unsaved spend their time.

Daily Salvations Require Daily Evangelism

"The Lord added to their number daily those who were being saved" (Acts 2:47). Pastors give altar calls after preaching on Sundays and Wednesdays, but in the New Testament church, people were getting saved on a daily basis. How can this happen in today's church unless every church member is witnessing on a daily basis?

We should imitate the early Christians who *"Day after day, in the temple courts and from house to house, they never stopped teaching and proclaiming the good news that Jesus is the Christ"* (Acts 5:42).

God is only limited by our imagination.

Imagine owning a fighter jet - and using it to drive to the grocery store. Christians have all the power in the universe at our disposal, yet we only wield it to heal a stubbed toe or to pay the rent. Sure, a jet could taxi down the road with wings scraping telephone poles and eventually make it to the store but this would be a serious waste of supersonic potential.

When a fighter pilot straps a jet to his back, he wants to travel at twice the speed of sound, not sit waiting at red lights. It is time to dream big, travel fast, and use God's power to the fullest.

How to be a good friend.

James Kennedy said, "Too often "friendship evangelism" never gets beyond friendship. Ofttimes the believer is content to "witness" with his exemplary lifestyle, assuming that someday, somehow, his friend will ask him how to come to Christ. Or he gets so caught up in the friendship that he fears threatening it by broadcasting it by broaching the subject of the Gospel."

It is time to aggressively make sure the people we call friends are going to heaven. Your relationships are bridges designed to bring people into contact with God.

Today's Temperature Forecast

Heaven   70 degrees

Hell   10,666 degrees

Where do you want to spend eternity?

Put your money where your heart is.

Your checkbook reveals your priorities. If you spent ten minutes looking at this month's financial statement would it expose your apathy or confirm your passion for soul winning?

What is more important:
* Changing your oil, or changing lives?
* Feeding yourself, or feeding the spiritually hungry?
* Investing in retirement, or investing in eternity?
* Paying your debt to the mortgage company, or paying your debt to God?

Don't curse the darkness when you can light a candle.

I was touring a cave with my family. The guide, wanting to duplicate the conditions the original explorer experienced, turned off all the lights. It was DARK! The guide lit a small flame and to my surprise, it lit up the entire cave. The world is a dark place, but all it takes is one light to make a big difference. Will you be that shining light?

"Let your light shine before men, that they may see your good deeds and praise your Father in heaven" (Matthew 5:16).

Ask, and it shall be given you

Do you ever feel like your passion for reaching the lost is lacking? Do you yawn during the missionary's slide show? Have you ever put a dollar in the offering just because you have to? If you feel guilty about not caring enough, ask God to give you a new passion for souls.

Go ahead, take a moment to pray and ask God to fill your heart with the same love for the lost that fills His heart. *"Ask of me, and I shall give thee the heathen for thine inheritance, and the uttermost parts of the earth for thy possession"* (Psalm 2:8 - KJV).

Three Things God Wants:

Our TIME
Our TALENT
Our TREASURE

Are you giving back to the One who gave to you?

Don't put on your swimming suit when God says "Walk on the Water"

Peter, seeing Jesus walking on the water called out, "Lord, if it is you, command me to come out on the water." Jesus replied with one simple word, "Come." On the basis of ONE WORD from Jesus, Peter defied the laws of gravity. Because of ONE WORD, Peter stepped out of the boat and into the pages of the Bible. With faith in ONE WORD, Peter stood up and took action.

ONE WORD from God will change your life forever.

God loves multitudes.

Some people say, "God is not interested in numbers." They fail to realize that God has an entire book named Numbers. They say, "We don't want quantity, we want quality." But God wants quantity with quality. You don't have to make a choice between them, you can have both. If you don't care about numbers, you don't care about people. For you to say you are not interested in numbers is to say to Tom, Dick, and Sally, "Go to Hell." Every number represents a soul.
- Billy Joe Daugherty

Power Evangelism

A flashlight without batteries is like a Christian without the Holy Spirit. Jesus promised, *"You will receive power when the Holy Spirit comes on you; and you will be my witnesses..."* (Acts 1:8). It is the power of the Holy Spirit which enables us to be shining lights all over the world.

> "Until you are filled with the Holy Spirit, don't go.
> After you are filled with the Holy Spirit, don't stay."
> - P.J. Titus

Witnesses everywhere!

Jesus said, "...You will be my witnesses in Jerusalem, and in all Judea and Samaria, and to the ends of the earth" (Acts 1:8).

Jerusalem was the city the disciples lived in,
            are you witnessing in your city?

Judea was the disciple's county,
            are you changing your country?

Samaria was a neighboring country,
            are you reaching out to other countries?

        The earth is a globe. Does a round shape like a globe have an end? No! If you start in your home town and begin traveling, you will never reach the end of the earth. This means we are supposed to go everywhere and tell everyone about Jesus...and we are never supposed to stop. *"You are my witnesses,"* declares the LORD, *"that I am God"* (Isaiah 43:12).

If we do not try to win souls, we will be held responsible for their loss.

"When I say to a wicked man, 'You will surely die,' and you do not warn him or speak out to dissuade him from his evil ways in order to save his life, that wicked man will die for his sin, and I will hold you accountable for his blood. But if you do warn the wicked man and he does not turn from his wickedness or from his evil ways, he will die for his sin; but you will have saved yourself" (Ezekiel 3:18-19).

The word "gospel" means "good news."

What is good news to the sinner?	Jesus can save you!
What is good news to the sick?	Jesus can heal you!
What is good news to the captive?	Jesus can set you free!
What is good news to the depressed?	Jesus can give you joy!
What is good news to the poor?	Jesus can make you rich!

Evangelists count people because people count.

Some imply that you can not measure the success of a ministry based on numbers, but I think it all depends on what numbers you are counting. If you are counting the number of people who heard the Gospel for the first time, the number of people saved, the number of people healed, and the number of believers inspired to do great things, then numbers are important. Each number represents a life changed for eternity.

Why do I believe in mass crusade evangelism? In these last days, a sickle can not keep up with the massive harvest, we need a combine machine. Why use a fishing rod when we can cast a net?

> **"Evangelism is usually a process of repeated exposure to the Good News."** - Rick Warren

Advertising executives know it takes an average of seven positive contacts with a product before someone uses it. Recently a new drink hit the market. I saw three advertisements for it on TV, I heard a radio ad, a friend mentioned he liked it, I noticed a display at a store, and the label on the bottle caught my attention before I decided to try the drink. Not one of these encounters was strong enough on its own to make me want the new drink, but when combined, they influenced me to buy. Often, it takes more than one truth encounter before someone is willing to dedicate his or her life to Christ. If someone does not get saved immediately, don't get discouraged...keep witnessing.

It is not our responsibility to bring all people to Christ, but to bring Christ to all people.

*"Swing the sickle, for the harvest is ripe...
Multitudes, multitudes in the valley of decision!"*
(Joel 3:13-14).

The harvest is ripe, but the workers are few. The threshing machines have rusted, the sickles are lost, and the barn has a hole in the roof. The sun is shining, the grain is ready to eat, but the fields are empty of workers. The farmers are still busy cleaning last year's harvest. They are counting, organizing, reporting, and rearranging instead of reaping.

How great is the Great Commission?

The Great Commission will require every Christian, every resource, and every bit of creativity the church can muster. We can not change the world by ignoring it. We can not fulfill the Great Commission by giving mediocre offerings nor by sending average individuals overseas. The Great Commission demands our best - our best talents, our best ideas, our best offerings, and our best young people.

The church is a training ground for battle against the forces of evil, not just a refuge from the storms of life.

The battle is great but the soldiers are absent without leave. Armor is rusted, swords are unpolished, and shields are full of holes. Marching orders have been ignored, the commander's voice is not recognized, and the officers are so busy mending injured soldiers that they cannot command the battle.

Christians are a mighty army. It is time to advance and attack. We must not retreat or stand still. An attacking army is a winning army. For the army of God, defense is not an option. For too long, we have been retreating in the face of Satan's attack. No longer! The devil must be put on the run.

Are you minding your own business or going about your Father's business?

Evangelizing is simply advertising, training disciples is like multi-level marketing, church is a sales training seminar, leading someone to the Lord is making a sale, and going to heaven is retirement.

The marketplace is ready. Our product is of infinite value, and its free! But God's salesmen are letting Him down. We peddle trivial trinkets instead of truth. We wonder why doodads and shiny contraptions fail to please hungry shoppers. We possess living water and the bread of life but all too often we only offer people moist towellets and small crumbs.

Loving God comes first, winning souls is a close second.

The greatest commandment is to love God with all your heart, mind, soul, and strength. The second greatest commandment is *"love your neighbor as you love yourself"* (Luke 10:27).

Our #1 purpose for being here on earth is to worship God. Our #2 purpose is to help other people discover their #1 purpose for being on earth.

The first instruction Jesus gave his disciples was *"Come, follow me"* (Mark 1:17). The last command he gave them was *"Go and make disciples"* (Matthew 28:19).

Jesus said, "I will make you fishers of men" (Mark 1:17).

"The difference between catching men and catching fish is that
you catch fish that are alive and they die,
you catch men that are dead and bring them to life."
- Dawson Trautman

What's the secret to soul winning?

Love God.

Love People.

Souls are eternal

"He that winneth souls is wise," because he has selected a wise object. I think it was Michelangelo who once carved certain magnificent statues in snow. They are gone; the material readily compacted by the frost as readily melted in the heat. Far wiser was he when he fashioned the enduring marble, and produced works which will last all down the ages. But even marble itself is consumed and fretted by the tooth of time; and he is wise who selects for his raw material immortal souls, whose existence shall outlast the stars."

- Charles Spurgeon

Preaching with Purpose

The purpose of preaching is not to impress the crowds with your wisdom, or your use of big words, or to make them laugh at your funny stories. The goal is to convince men and woman of the truth and to lead them to the Savior. Anything less is a waste of your breath and their time.

"The preaching of the Gospel minister should always have soulwinning for its object."
- Charles Spurgeon

What makes God happy?

I may be a little biased but I think being an evangelist is the best job in the universe. Jesus said, *"I tell you...there will be more rejoicing in heaven over one sinner who repents than over ninety-nine righteous persons who do not need to repent"* (Luke 15:7). Pastoring churches is great, teaching the saints is wonderful, but God's greatest joy is when a sinner is saved.

If you listen closely to the heartbeat of God, you will hear the rhythmic beat,

"Souls...Souls...Souls...Souls..."

Oh, that our hearts would beat with the same cadence.

How far does your light shine?

Some ask, "Why should I be concerned with world evangelism when there are so many people nearby who are still unsaved?"

Oswald J. Smith answers, "Why should anyone hear the gospel twice before everyone has heard it once?"

The light that shine farthest shines brightest near at home. In my experience, those who are most excited about evangelism in their own neighborhoods are those who have a heart for the whole world.

7 Reasons to Be a Soul Winner

Reason #1: The Bible commands it

"He said to them, "Go into all the world and preach the good news to all creation" (Mark 16:15).

This is the Great Commission, not just a good suggestion. What do you think God meant when he said "Go"?

"The Great Commission is not an option to be considered, it is a command to be obeyed." - J. Hudson Taylor

Reason #2: Love compels it

"Christ's love compels us...All this is from God, who reconciled us to himself through Christ and gave us the ministry of reconciliation: that God was reconciling the world to himself in Christ, not counting men's sins against them. And he has committed to us the message of reconciliation. We are therefore Christ's ambassadors..." (2 Corinthians 5:14;18-20).

Because of Christ's love, we are ministers of reconciliation (bringing God and man together) and ambassadors of Christ (representing God to humankind).

Reason #3: The harvest demands it.

"Do you not say, 'Four months more and then the harvest'? I tell you, open your eyes and look at the fields! They are ripe for harvest" (John 4:35).

The harvest is only ripe for a season before it is lost. There is a short window of time to reach people and we must take full advantage of the opportunity. We share the gospel so the harvest will be reaped.

36

Reason #4: The world needs it

"The dark places of the earth are full of the habitations of cruelty" (Psalm 74:20).

Any place which has not heard of Jesus is filled with cruel traditions, abusive situations, and unspeakable horror. People do terrible things to one another when they are without God. Only the gospel can change the hearts and minds of those controlled by Satan.

Reason #5: Someone pleads for it

"During the night Paul had a vision of a man of Macedonia standing and begging him, "Come over to Macedonia and help us" (Acts 16:9).

Paul was wondering where he should go to minister when this man appeared to him begging for help. In response to the desperate cry, Paul went to the city of Philippi in the province of Macedonia and established a church.

Right now, someone is pleading for your help. If you will listen with your spiritual ears, you will hear the cry of lost souls who need you.

Reason #6: Compassion requires it

"When [Jesus] saw the crowds, he had compassion on them, because they were harassed and helpless, like sheep without a shepherd" (Matthew 9:36).

Jesus had compassion because his Father had compassion (Psalm 86:15). We should have compassion on the lost because Jesus had compassion on us when we were lost.

Reason #7: Christ's return depends on it

"This gospel of the kingdom will be preached in the whole world as a testimony to all nations, and then the end will come" (Matthew 24:14).

Do you want Jesus to return? The timetable for his return rests in the hands of the church. As soon as we complete the task he gave us, he will come back for us.

Destiny begins with being a servant

D.L. Moody explained, "There are many of us that are willing to do great things for the Lord, but few of us are willing to do little things."

Jesus said, *"Well done, good and faithful servant! You have been faithful with a few things; I will put you in charge of many things. Come and share your master's happiness!"* (Matthew 25:21).

If you want to do something great for God, begin by winning the souls around you and God will eventually promote you to a greater position of influence.

Before you can be a fisher, you must be a follower.

"Come, follow me," Jesus said, *"and I will make you fishers of men."* (Matthew 4:19).

Instructions must be obeyed in the proper sequence. Your ministry begins when you forsake the world and follow Christ. If you are not wholeheartedly following Jesus, you will not catch any lost souls. As Charles Spurgeon said, "The worldly Christian will not convert the world...If you march with the armies of the Wicked One, you cannot defeat them. I believe that one reason why the church of God at this present moment has so little influence over the world is because the world has so much influence over the church."

Are you wise?

"He who wins souls is wise"
(Proverbs 11:30).

The Bible does not say, "He who makes money is wise" or "She who writes bestselling books is wise" or "He who preaches is wise" or even "Those who talk about soul winning are wise." Only those who are actually leading the lost to Christ are wise. Do you qualify?

Your money makes a difference in eternity.

"Everyone who calls on the name of the Lord will be saved." How, then, can they call on the one they have not believed in? And how can they believe in the one of whom they have not heard? And how can they hear without someone preaching to them? And how can they preach unless they are sent? (Romans 10:13-15).

In order for the today's preacher to be sent, someone must give money to help buy the plane ticket. Money is needed to pay for sound systems, television time, literature distribution, etc.

The salvation of a lost soul begins with the sound of money dropping in the offering bucket. Every penny represents a person, every nickel a need, every dollar a destiny.

39

Jesus is coming soon... sooner than you think. Are you ready?

Is your neighbor ready?
Are the nations ready?
Will you be a part of God's grand finale?

"I looked for a man among them who would...stand before me in the gap on behalf of the land..." (Ezekiel 22:30).

"I heard the voice of the Lord saying, "Whom shall I send?...And I said, "Here am I. Send me!" (Isaiah 6:8).

"Look at the nations and watch, and be utterly amazed. For I am going to do something in your days that you would not believe, even if you were told" (Habakkuk 1:5).

People of every color will worship before the throne.

"This gospel of the kingdom will be preached in the whole world as a testimony to all nations, and then the end will come" (Matthew 24:14).

The word "nations" used in this verse is the Greek word *ethnos* which is where we get our word "ethnic." It refers to every people group, language group, and cultural group in the world.

"And they sang a new song: "You are worthy to take the scroll and to open its seals, because you were slain, and with your blood you purchased men for God from every tribe and language and people and nation" (Revelation 5:9).

Pray for the Harvest Fields

"When Jesus saw the multitudes, he was moved with compassion for them...Then he said to his disciples, The harvest truly is plenteous, but the labourers are few; Pray ye therefore the Lord of the harvest, that he will send forth labourers into his harvest" (Matthew 9:36 - KJV).

Jesus commanded the disciples to pray for laborers. I believe they obeyed because in the very next verse (Matthew 10:1), their prayers are answered when Jesus commissions the disciples for ministry. This means the disciples became the answer to their own prayers. When you begin to pray for the harvest fields, God will open up the door for you to become a laborer in the harvest fields.

It is time to wake up, Church!

"If you found a cure for cancer it would be inconceivable to hide it from the rest of mankind. How much more inconceivable to keep silent the cure from the eternal wages of death." - Dave Davidson

"Today a jumbo jet can be hijacked with 80 people on board. An event such as this would grab headlines the world over. The fact that millions are held hostage by eternal darkness, with hell being their plight, is barely mentioned by the body of Christ today." - Mike Francen

Are you praying hard,
or hardly praying?

I agree with Gordon Lindsay, "Every person ought to pray at least one violent prayer every day."

Prayer does not need a passport. There are no "closed countries" when it comes to the power of prayer.

Soul winning depends more on the calluses on your knees then the genus of your plans.

"The great tragedy in of life is not unanswered prayer, but unoffered prayer." - F.B. Myer

Our GOAL? Every SOUL!

"All that is not eternal is eternally out of date." - C.S. Lewis

"The devil want you to do good, because doing good will keep you from doing God's best. And God's best is souls."
- Lester Sumrall

"If you keep souls your number one priority you will never be out of the will of God." - Lester Sumrall

How to Lead Someone to the Lord.

1. Look for opportunities to share the Gospel.

Sharing Christ is like one starving man who found bread telling another starving man where to find it. No matter where you go, you are surrounded by people who need Jesus. Where are these people?

- At work   - Relatives   - Waitresses
- Next door   - Fellow students   - Store Clerks
- Friends   - On an airline flight   - The mission field

Jesus witnessed to the woman at the well (John 4), Andrew brought his brother Peter to Jesus (John 1), Philip brought Nathaniel (John 1), Peter witnessed to the cripple at the temple gate (Acts 3), and Paul witnessed to his jailer (Acts 16). Find someone who needs Jesus and start witnessing.

2. Initiate a conversation about God.

According to Bill Hybels, "Evangelism should be as natural as breathing." It does not have to be scary or hard. Witnessing is simply an overflow of what God has done for you.

Opening questions:

Would you like to hear some Good News? Is Jesus the Lord of your life? If you died tonight, would you go to heaven? How is your relationship with God? Another great way to stir up interest is to share your own testimony. You could say, "Did you know that just five years ago, I was a mean, good-for-nothing, lying and stealing person but now I'm one of the nicest people you'll ever meet? Do you want to know what happened to me?

3. Present the Gospel message.

A. God loves you.
"God is love" (1 John 4:8).
"For God so loved the world that he gave his one and only Son, that whoever believes in him shall not perish but have eternal life" (John 3:16).

B. Sin separates us from God.
"All have sinned and fall short of the glory of God" (Romans 3:23).
"For the wages of sin is death, but the gift of God is eternal life in Christ Jesus our Lord" (Romans 6:23).

C. Jesus died on the cross to pay the price for our sins.
"Christ died for our sins according to the Scriptures...he was buried...he was raised on the third day" (1 Corinthians 15:3-4).
"The blood of Jesus...purifies us from all sin" (1 John 1:7).

D. You can be saved.
"If you confess with your mouth, "Jesus is Lord," and believe in your heart that God raised him from the dead, you will be saved" (Romans 10:9).
"If we confess our sins, he is faithful and just and will forgive us our sins and purify us from all unrighteousness" (1 John 1:9).

4. Ask for commitment
Ask "Would you like to make Jesus the Lord of your life? Would you be willing to pray with me right now?" Pray this prayer: "Dear Heavenly Father, I ask forgiveness for all my sins. I believe Jesus died on the cross to pay for my sins. I believe He rose from the dead and right now I invite him to be Lord of my life. Amen." After praying together, ask your new family member to go to church with you.

S.O.S.

In Morse code, S.O.S. means "Save Our Souls." It is used when a ship is sinking. Every ship within radio distance of this call immediately changes course in order to help. Right now, if you listen, masses of people are silently screaming "S.O.S."

While you have been reading this book, 7,000 souls have gone to hell.

Your dollar, given to missions, is a life jacket for a drowning soul, your message is a lifeline to someone going down for the third time, your prayers are lifeboats for the lost.

Will you change course to save lost souls?

"God, I pray, light these idle sticks of my life and may I burn up for Thee. Consume my life, my God, for it is Thine. I seek not a long life but a full one like Yours, Lord Jesus" - Jim Elliot

"The Great Commission is still in effect.
Christ's command has not changed,
and neither has God's great plan of redemption."
- Billy Graham

"Our Ambition - The Great Commission!" -Reinhard Bonnke

Soul Winning

The Million Heirs Club is a group of people, like you, who are passionate about soul winning and have committed to help Daniel King win 1,000,000 souls every year.

How did the Million Heirs Club get started?

When I was fifteen years old, I was reading a success book. One of its keys to success was writing down goals. One particular goal the book mentioned caught my eye. It said many young people make it a goal to earn $1,000,000 before the age of 30. I thought about making that a goal for my life but because of my upbringing as a missionary in Mexico, I realized money was not important to me. Instead, I wrote down this goal, "I want to win 1,000,000 people to Jesus before I turn 30." Instead of trying to become a millionaire, I decided to win a million "heirs" to the kingdom of God.

"If you belong to Christ, then you...are heirs" (Galatians 3:29).

Once I completed my initial goal of leading one million people to Jesus, I decided to make it a yearly goal to win at least a million souls for heaven through massive miracle crusades, leadership training, literature distribution, and practical relief.

What are the benefits of joining the Million Heirs Club?

1. You are investing in eternity.
2. Every dollar you give results in approximately one soul saved.
3. You receive a Million Heirs Club certificate to hang on your wall.
4. Periodically throughout the year, you receive newsletters, ministry updates, and gifts from Daniel King.
5. You will be given VIP invitations to join us in ministry events around the world.
6. You will become a heavenly millionaire!

How can you join the Million Heirs Club?

Commit to give at least $30 each month
to help King Ministries win souls.

What are the different levels of Million Heirs Club members?

Member: Give at least $30 every month
Bronze Level Crusade Sponsor (Contribute $1000-$10,000)
Silver Level Crusade Sponsor (City-Wide Event) $25,000
Gold Level Crusade Sponsor (Regional Event) $50,000
Platinum Level Crusade Sponsor (National Event) $100,000

There are three ways to become a **Lifetime Member** of the Million Heirs Club:
1. Give $1,000,000 to help Daniel King evangelize the world.
2. Pray one million minutes for souls to be saved
(1 hour a day for forty-six years).
3. Lead one million people in a salvation prayer.

Yes! I want to join the Million Heir's Club and help Daniel King win 1,000,000 souls to Jesus every year.

Name: _____

Address: _____

State: _____ Zip Code: _____

Phone: _____

E-mail: _____

Enclosed is my gift of:

$100 $50 $500 $1,000   Other: _____

Yes! I want to make a monthly pledge of $ _____

Please charge my: VISA or MASTERCARD (Circle One)

__ __ __ - __ __ __ __ - __ __ __ __ - __ __ __ __

Expiration Date: __ __ / __ __ Signature: _____

If you want to become a member of the Million Heirs Club, fill out this page and mail it to:

King Ministries International
P.O. Box 370056
El Paso, TX 79937

About the Author:

Daniel King is in high demand as a speaker at churches and conferences all over America. His passion, energy, and enthusiasm are enjoyed by audiences everywhere he goes.

Daniel is an international evangelist who does massive miracle crusades in countries around the world. His passion for the lost has taken him to over forty nations preaching the gospel to crowds which often exceed 50,000 people.

He was called into the ministry when he was five years old and began to preach when he was six. His parents became missionaries to Mexico when he was ten. When he was fourteen he started a children's ministry which gave him the opportunity to minister in some of America's largest churches while he was still a teenager.

At the age of fifteen, Daniel read a book where the author encouraged young people to set a goal to earn $1,000,000. Daniel reinterpreted the message and determined to win 1,000,000 people to Christ every year.

Daniel has authored eight books including his best-sellers "Healing Power" and "Fire Power." His book "Welcome to the Kingdom" has been given away to thousands of new believers.

The vision of **King Ministries** is
to bring 1,000,000 souls into the kingdom
of God every year and to train believers to
become leaders.

If you want Daniel King
to visit your church, write:

King Ministries
PO Box 701113
Tulsa, OK 74170-1113 USA

or call toll-free:
1-877-431-4276

or visit us on-line at:
www.kingministries.com

Books by Daniel King

Healing Power
"This is the best book I have ever read on healing." - Mike Murdock

"I loved this book and I think you will, too." - Marilyn Hickey

Fire Power
"Daniel King is a young man on fire for God." - Billy Joe Daugherty

"In this book, Daniel shares how he keeps his "red-hot" relationship with God." - Charles Nieman

The Power of the Seed
"...I was impressed with the understanding Daniel has on this subject." - Robb Thompson

"...Interesting read as well as being a great text book on the Seed..." - John Avanzini

Soul Winning
"I have seen Daniel King in action and the book exudes the same passion for people that you notice when you spend time with the author." - Peter Youngren

Welcome to the Kingdom is the perfect book to give to new believers Call and ask about bulk discounts.

To order Daniel's books call toll-free:
1-877-431-4276